Not Just MORE Socks

Sandi Rosner

Editorial Director   David Codling

Editor and Graphic Design   Gregory Courtney

Photography   Kathryn Martin

Makeup and Hair Styling   Kira Lee

Clothing Stylist   Betsy Westman

Models   Emily Fahey, Joel Broderick, Michelle Rich, "Higgins" and "Pursuit"

Special Thanks   Anne Takemoto

Color Reproduction and Printing   Regent Publishing Services

Published and Distributed By   Unicorn Books and Crafts, Inc.

Printed in China

ISBN   1-893063-13-5

1 2 3 4 5 6 7 8 9 10

UNICORN
BOOKS AND CRAFTS, INC.

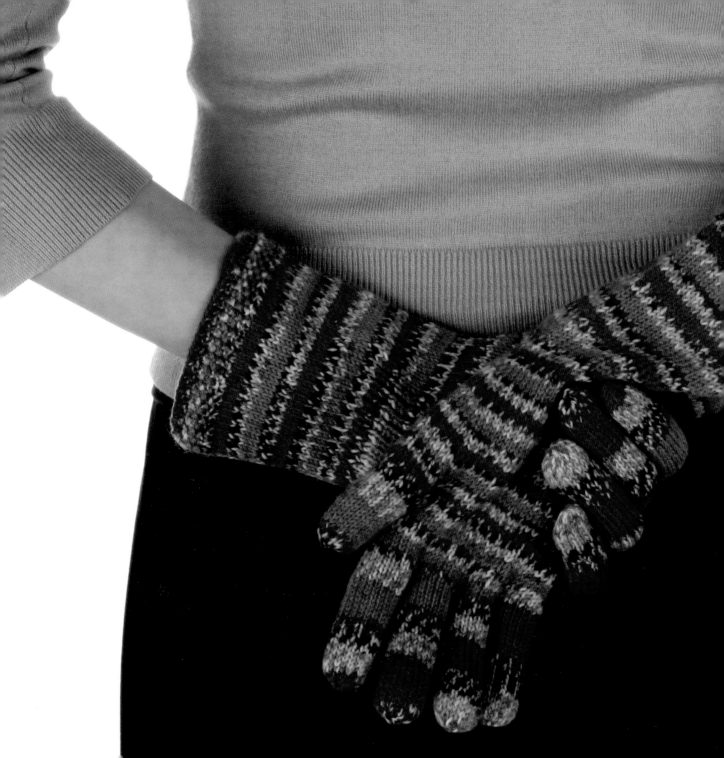

Introduction

The popularity of the original **Not Just Socks**, released only last year, has been phenomenal. Who knew so many knitters were working with self-striping sock yarns? This expanded collection continues to explore the possibilities of these popular yarns, using some old favorites and introducing new stripe styles now available.

While **Not Just Socks** used mostly basic stitches, the patterns in this book take advantage of more complex techniques and unusual construction methods to exploit the color changes in self-striping yarns. That said, the projects are still within the reach of all but the newest of beginners. While the patterns use common techniques found in any good knitting reference, some may be new to you. There are many good "how to knit" books available and no knitting library is complete without one.

Jump in and try something new. Self-striping yarns can make every knitter look like an expert. You'll love the results and your friends will marvel at your ingenuity.

Thoughts on Working with Self-striping Sock Yarns

〰 You don't have to use the colors in your yarn in the order they appear. Feel free to manipulate the color placement to please yourself. If you want green thumbs on your mittens, just wind off some yarn until you get to the green section. If you want your ribbed edges in a solid color, just wind off the spotted part.

〰 Pay attention to the sequence of colors in your yarn. If you want the pieces of a pair to match, you will want to make sure the colors appear in the same order. When you start a new ball of yarn, make sure the colors run in the same direction. Rarely, but sometimes, the sequence will reverse from skein to skein, even within the same dye lot. You may need to work one skein from the outside and the next from the inside strand in order to keep the sequence consistent.

〰 Some people love the look of an unmatched pair. For others, it just makes them crazy. You know who you are. If you want your pair to match, start the first piece at the junction between two colors. Wind off yarn to get to the same place in the color sequence when you start the second piece. If an unmatched look is more your style, just start wherever you are and let the colors fall as they may. Both approaches are reflected in the projects in this book.

〰 Remember that tiny changes in tension will affect how the colors in your yarn line up, particularly in the spotted sections. The spots may stack in one stripe, and form chevrons in another. Don't make yourself nuts trying to control this. Embrace serendipity! Allow your project to delight you with its idiosyncrasies.

〰 Stripe styles and colorways change each season, with some being discontinued to make room for new favorites. If you can't find the exact yarn used in the book, choose your favorite colors from the selection at your local yarn store. The length of the color stretches and proportion of solid color to speckles will affect the look of your project. The staff in your yarn shop should be able to tell you how a particular ball of yarn will work up so you can make a choice that will please you.

Hats

Hats

Hats

Hats

Hats

Bias Hat

DIFFICULTY INTERMEDIATE

YARN LANA GROSSA FANTASY (100 GRAMS)

NEEDLES 16" CIRCULAR AND SET OF FOUR DOUBLE-POINTED US 2 (2.75 MM) *OR THE SIZE YOU NEED TO GET GAUGE*

SIZE ADULT MEDIUM
MEASUREMENTS 21" CIRCUMFERENCE

GAUGE 28 STS AND 36 ROWS = 4" IN STOCKINETTE STITCH

Here is an alternative to the basic beanie shape. The body of this hat shows the stripes at an angle, while the top is finished with a five-pointed star.

Body of Hat
Using waste yarn and circular needle, CO 45 sts. Change to main yarn and work as follows:

Row 1 (WS): Sl 1, K9, P to end of row.
Row 2 (RS): K1, K2tog, K32, m1, K10.

Repeat these two rows until piece measures 21" (or desired head circumference) measured along the edge opposite the garter stitch border. Remove waste yarn. As you pick out the waste yarn stitch by stitch, you will free the bottom loops of your first row of knitting. Place these new stitches on one of your double-pointed needles. Graft the ends of your strip together using the kitchener stitch.

Crown
Using 16" circular needle, pick up 160 sts evenly along edge of strip opposite garter stitch border. K 2 rounds.

Shape Crown
Round 1: * K14, dbl dec, K15, repeat from * to end of round.
Round 2 and all even numbered rounds: K.
Round 3: * K13, dbl dec, K14, repeat from * to end of round.
Round 5: * K12, dbl dec, K13, repeat from * to end of round.
Round 7: * K11, dbl dec, K12, repeat from * to end of round.
Round 9: * K10, dbl dec, K11, repeat from * to end of round.
Round 11: * K9, dbl dec, K10, repeat from * to end of round.

Change to double-pointed needles.

Round 13: * K8, dbl dec, K9, repeat from * to end of round.
Round 15: * K7, dbl dec, K8, repeat from * to end of round.
Round 17: * K6, dbl dec, K7, repeat from * to end of round.
Round 19: * K5, dbl dec, K6, repeat from * to end of round.
Round 21: * K4, dbl dec, K5, repeat from * to end of round.
Round 23: * K3, dbl dec, K4, repeat from * to end of round.
Round 25: * K2, dbl dec, K3, repeat from * to end of round.
Round 27: * K1, dbl dec, K2, repeat from * to end of round.
Round 28: * Dbl dec, K1, repeat from * to end of round.

Break yarn, draw through remaining 10 sts, pull tight and fasten off.

Finishing
Weave in ends. Steam lightly, stretching garter stitch brim a bit and smoothing out the crown.

TIP
If you're having trouble picking up just the right number of stitches, pick up one stitch for every row. Figure out how many you need to increase or decrease to get to the correct number. On the first row, scatter the increases or decreases more or less evenly around. So long as you get to the correct number of stitches before starting the crown shaping, you'll be fine.

Jughead's Hat

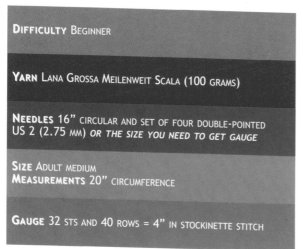

DIFFICULTY BEGINNER

YARN LANA GROSSA MEILENWEIT SCALA (100 GRAMS)

NEEDLES 16" CIRCULAR AND SET OF FOUR DOUBLE-POINTED US 2 (2.75 MM) *OR THE SIZE YOU NEED TO GET GAUGE*

SIZE ADULT MEDIUM
MEASUREMENTS 20" CIRCUMFERENCE

GAUGE 32 STS AND 40 ROWS = 4" IN STOCKINETTE STITCH

Brim Triangles (Make 6)
CO 39 sts.

Row 1 and all WS rows: Sl 1, K to last st, sl 1.
Row 2: SSK, K16, dbl dec, K16, K2tog.
Row 4: SSK, K14, dbl dec, K14, K2tog.
Row 6: SSK, K12, dbl dec, K12, K2tog.
Row 8: SSK, K10, dbl dec, K10, K2tog.
Row 10: SSK, K8, dbl dec, K8, K2tog.
Row 12: SSK, K6, dbl dec, K6, K2tog.
Row 14: SSK, K4, dbl dec, K4, K2tog.
Row 16: SSK, K2, dbl dec, K2, K2tog.
Row 18: SSK, dbl dec, K2tog.
Row 19: Sl 1, K1, P1.
Row 20: Sl 1, K2tog, psso.

Break yarn and fasten off last stitch.

Body of Hat
With circular needle and RS facing, pick up and knit 20 sts along base of

each triangle, joining triangles together as you go. *DO NOT JOIN INTO A CIRCLE.*

Next row: * P2, P into front and back of next st, repeat from * to end of row—160 sts.

Place a marker to indicate beginning of round and join into a circle, with WS of triangles facing out. Purl 10 rounds.

Next round: * K80, m1, repeat from * once more—162 sts.

Work in st st for 4".

Shape Crown
Set up round: * K27, pm, repeat from * to end of round—6 markers placed.

Decrease round: * K to 2 sts before marker, K2tog, repeat from * to end of round.

Continue in st st, working decrease round every other round until 90 sts remain. Discontinue plain rounds and work decrease round every round until 12 sts remain, changing to double-pointed needles when necessary.

TIP
The slipped stitches at the beginning and end of the wrong side rows make a tidy chain edge. Slip the stitches as if to purl with yarn in front. When you pick up stitches along this edge, it's easy to pick up one stitch in each link of the chain.

Break yarn and draw through remaining 12 sts. Pull tight and fasten off.

Finishing
Fold triangles upwards and secure cuff by sewing base of triangles to top row of purl sts. Weave in ends. Block gently.

The points around the brim are reminiscent of the hat worn by Jughead, the faithful sidekick in the old Archie comics! Use a bright or light color on the cast-on edge of the triangles to make them stand out.

Beret

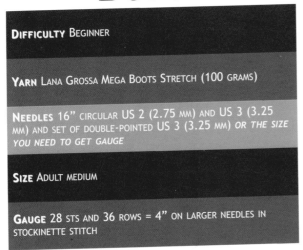

DIFFICULTY BEGINNER

YARN LANA GROSSA MEGA BOOTS STRETCH (100 GRAMS)

NEEDLES 16" CIRCULAR US 2 (2.75 MM) AND US 3 (3.25 MM) AND SET OF DOUBLE-POINTED US 3 (3.25 MM) *OR THE SIZE YOU NEED TO GET GAUGE*

SIZE ADULT MEDIUM

GAUGE 28 STS AND 36 ROWS = 4" ON LARGER NEEDLES IN STOCKINETTE STITCH

Wear this classic shape at a jaunty angle. This beret is most effective when knitted in yarns designed to produce a broad stripe.

Beret

With smaller circular needle, loosely CO 120 sts. Join into the round, being careful not to twist your sts. Work in K1 P1 ribbing for 1½". Change to larger needles.

Next rnd (increase round): * K2, m1, repeat from * to end of round—180 sts.

Continue in st st without further shaping until piece measures 6" from beginning.

Shape Crown

Set-up round: * K30, pm, repeat from * to end of round—6 markers placed.

Decrease round: * K to 2 sts before marker, K2tog, slip marker, repeat from * to end of round.

Repeat decrease round until 6 sts remain, changing to double-pointed needles when necessary. Break yarn, draw through remaining sts, pull tight and fasten off. Make a pompon and sew to the top of your beret. Weave in ends. Block gently.

TIP
Berets take on their characteristic flat shape when blocked around a dinner plate. Put the plate inside your hat, centering the top of the hat on the back of the plate. Steam gently. Remove the plate when the beret is completely dry.

Gloves & Mittens

Gloves & Mittens

Gloves & Mittens

Gloves & Mittens

Gloves & Mittens

Sawtooth Mittens

DIFFICULTY INTERMEDIATE

YARN LANA GROSSA MEILENWEIT MAGICO (100 GRAMS)

NEEDLES SET OF 4 DOUBLE-POINTED US 2 (2.75 MM) OR THE SIZE YOU NEED TO GET GAUGE.

SIZE WOMEN'S MEDIUM (MEN'S MEDIUM)
MEASUREMENTS 8" (9") HAND CIRCUMFERENCE AROUND PALM ABOVE THUMB

GAUGE 32 STS AND 40 ROWS = 4" IN STOCKINETTE STITCH

Inner Cuff
CO 10 sts.

Row 1 (RS): K7, yo, K3.
Row 2 and all WS rows: K.
Row 3: K7, yo, K4.
Row 5: K7, yo, K5.
Row 7: K7, yo, K6.
Row 9: K7, yo, K7.
Row 11: K7, yo, K8.
Row 13: K7, yo, K9—17 sts.
Row 14: BO 7, K to end—10 sts.

Change color. Repeat rows 1-14 five (six) times more, changing color before row 1 each time. BO remaining 10 sts. Sew bound-off edge to cast-on edge, forming a ring. Set aside.

Outer Cuff
CO 6 sts.

Row 1 (RS): K3, yo, K3.
Row 2 and all WS rows: K.
Row 3: K3, yo, K4.
Row 5: K3, yo, K5.
Row 7: K3, yo, K6.
Row 9: K3, yo, K7.
Row 11: K3, yo, K8.
Row 13: K3, yo, K9—13 sts.
Row 14: BO 7, K to end—6 sts.

Change color. Repeat rows 1-14 five (six) times more, changing color before row 1 each time. BO remaining 6 sts. Sew bound-off edge to cast-on edge, forming a ring. Place inner cuff inside outer cuff, lining up straight edges and offsetting the points as shown in photo. Working through both layers, pick up and knit 1 st in each ridge along straight edge—42 (49) sts. Arrange sts on 3 needles. Place marker to indicate beginning of round.

Next round - *smaller size* (inc by knitting in front and back of st): inc 1, * inc 1, K1, repeat from * to last st, ending with inc 1—64 sts; *larger size*: *k1, inc 1, rep from * to last 3 sts; ending with k3—72 sts.

Palm
Set-up round: K32 (36), pm, m1, pm, K32 (36).

Increase round: K to marker, sl marker, m1, K to marker, m1, sl marker, K to end of round.

Continue in st st, working increase round every 3rd round 10 (12) times—21 (25) sts between markers, 85 (97) sts total.

Next round: K to marker, remove marker, place gusset stitches on waste yarn for holding, remove marker, CO 1 st to bridge the gap, K to end of round—65 (73) sts.

Work even until palm measures 6" (7") above cuff, decreasing 1 st on last row.

Shape Top
Round 1: * K14 (16), K2tog, repeat from * 3 times more—60 (68) sts.
Round 2: K.

Repeat these two rounds, working one less st between decreases and decreasing 4 sts every other round, until 32 (36) sts remain. Then discontinue plain rounds and decrease 4 sts every round until 8 sts remain. Break yarn, draw through remaining 8 sts, pull tight and fasten off.

Thumb
Place held gusset sts on needles. Join yarn and pick up 1 st at palm—22 (26) sts. Arrange sts evenly on 3 needles and work until thumb measures 1¾" (2"). K2tog 11 (13) times.

Next round: K2tog 4 (5) times, K3tog.

Finishing
Break yarn and thread through remaining 5 sts. Pull tight and fasten off. Weave in ends and block to finished measurements.

TIP
When finishing the tip of your mitten or glove fingers, run the end of the yarn through the final few stitches twice, then pull tight. Two strands fill the stitches more completely and gives a better-looking result.

A double layer of sawtooth points makes warm and decorative cuffs for these mittens. The points are a great opportunity to play with the arrangement of colors in your yarn.

Button Gloves

DIFFICULTY INTERMEDIATE

YARN LANA GROSSA MEILENWEIT INCA (100 GRAMS)

NEEDLES SET OF 4 DOUBLE-POINTED US 1 (2.25) AND US 2 (2.75 MM) *OR THE SIZE YOU NEED TO GET GAUGE*

ACCESSORIES EIGHT 3/8" BUTTONS

SIZE WOMEN'S MEDIUM
MEASUREMENTS 8" HAND CIRCUMFERENCE AROUND PALM ABOVE THUMB

GAUGE 32 STS AND 40 ROWS = 4" IN STOCKINETTE STITCH

Seed Stitch

Row 1: * K1, P1, repeat from * to end of row.
Row 2: Knit the purl sts and purl the knit sts as they face you.

Left Glove

Cuff

With larger needles, CO 64 sts. Work in Seed Stitch for 1".

Next row (decrease row): K2, SSK, K to last 4 sts, K2tog, K2.

Continue in st st, working decrease row every 6th row 3 times more—56 sts.

Continue without shaping until piece measures 3½".

Next row: K6, (P1, K1) 7 times, P1, K to end of row.
Next row: P35, (K1, P1) 7 times, K1, P to end of row.

Repeat these two rows 5 times more.

Place all sts on a flexible holder. Use a spare circular needle or waste yarn to hold your sts.

Button Band

With smaller needles, starting at seed stitch end of cuff, with RS facing, pick up and knit 33 sts along side edge. Work in Seed Stitch for 10 rows. BO.

Buttonhole Band

With smaller needles, starting with held sts, with RS facing, pick up and knit 33 sts along side edge. Work 3 rows Seed Stitch.

Next row: K3, * K2tog, yo, K6, repeat from * twice more, end with K2tog, yo, K4.

Work 5 more rows seed st. BO.

Place held sts back on larger needles. Lay buttonhole band over button band, re-join yarn, and pick up and

knit 8 sts through both layers—64 sts. Place marker to indicate beginning of round. K 1 round.

Lower Palm

Set-up round: K32, pm, m1, pm, K32.

Increase round: K to marker, sl marker, m1, K to marker, m1, sl marker, K to end of round.

Continue in st st, working increase round every 3rd round 10 times—21 sts between markers, 85 sts total.

Next round: K to marker, remove marker, place gusset stitches on waste yarn for holding, remove marker, CO 1 st to bridge the gap, K to end of round—65 sts. Work even until palm measures 3¾" above ribbing.

Little Finger

K8, place next 50 sts on waste yarn, CO 2 sts to bridge the gap, K to end of round—17 sts. Arrange sts evenly on 3 needles and work until little finger measures 2¼" long.

Decrease and Finish Fingertip

K2tog 7 times, K3tog. Break yarn and thread through remaining 8 sts. Pull tight and fasten off.

TIP
Finger lengths vary quite a bit. If possible, have the intended wearer try on the gloves before finishing the fingers.

Upper Palm

Place held sts on needles and join yarn at base of little finger. Pick up 2 sts along CO edge at base of little finger—52 sts. Work in st st for 4 rounds.

Ring Finger

K9, place next 34 sts on waste yarn, CO 2 sts to bridge the gap, K9—20 sts. Arrange sts evenly on 3 needles and work until ring finger measures 2¾".

Decrease and Finish Fingertip
K2tog 10 times, K2tog 5 times. Break yarn and thread through remaining 5 sts. Pull tight and fasten off.

Middle Finger
Place held sts on needles and join yarn at the base of ring finger. K8, place next 18 sts on waste yarn, CO 2 sts to bridge the gap, K8, pick up 2 sts along CO edge at base of ring finger—20 sts. Arrange sts evenly on 3 needles and work until middle finger measures 3". Decrease and finish fingertip as for ring finger.

Index Finger
Place remaining sts on needles. Join yarn and pick up 2 sts along CO edge at base of middle finger—20 sts. Arrange sts evenly on 3 needles and work until index finger measures 2¾". Decrease and finish fingertip as for ring finger.

Thumb
Place held gusset sts on needles. Join yarn and pick up 1 st at palm—22 sts. Arrange sts evenly on 3 needles and work until thumb measures 2". K2tog 11 times. K2tog 4 times, K3tog. Break yarn and thread through remaining 5 sts. Pull tight and fasten off.

Right Glove
Cuff
With larger needles, CO 64 sts. Work in Seed Stitch for 1".

Next row (decrease row): K2, SSK, K to last 4 sts, K2tog, K2.

Continue in st st, working decrease row every 6th row 3 times more—56 sts.

> **TIP**
> *Leave a generous tail when joining yarn at the beginning of each finger. When you weave in these tails, use them to close up any little gaps that develop at the base of the fingers.*

Continue without shaping until piece measures 3½".

Next row: K35, (P1, K1) 7 times, P1, K to end of row.
Next row: P6, (K1, P1) 7 times, K1, P to end of row.

Repeat these two rows 5 times more.

Place all sts on a flexible holder. Use a spare circular needle or waste yarn to hold your sts.

Button Band
With smaller needles, starting with held sts, with RS facing, pick up and knit 33 sts along side edge. Work in Seed Stitch for 10 rows. BO.

Buttonhole Band
With smaller needles, starting at Seed Stitch end of cuff, with RS facing, pick up and knit 33 sts along side edge. Work 3 rows Seed Stitch.

Next row: K3, * K2tog, yo, K6, repeat from * twice more, end with K2tog, yo, K4.

Work 5 more rows in Seed Stitch. BO.

Place held sts back on larger needles. Lay buttonhole band over button band, place marker to indicate beginning of round, re-join yarn, and pick up and knit 8 sts through both layers—64 sts. K 1 round.

Continue as for left glove from lower palm instructions.

Finishing
Weave in ends. Sew buttons to button bands to correspond to buttonholes. Block to finished measurements.

These ladylike gloves have longer, buttoned cuffs for a dressy look.

Ridge Pattern
Row 1: K.
Row 2: Sl 1, P to last st, K1.
Row 3: Sl 1, P to last st, K1.
Row 4: Sl 1, K to end of row.
Row 5: Rep row 3.
Row 6: Rep row 4.
Row 7: Rep row 4.
Row 8: Rep row 3.
Row 9: Rep row 4.
Row 10: Rep row 3.

Wrist Warmers
Using waste yarn, CO 45 sts. Change to main yarn and work rows 1-10 of Ridge Pattern, then rep rows 3-10 until piece measures approximately 3" from beginning, ending with row 4.

Thumb Gusset
Row 1: K10, place these sts on holder, sl 1, P2, W&T, K to end.
Row 2: Sl 1, P4, W&T, K to end.
Row 3: Sl 1, P6, W&T, K to end.
Row 4: Sl 1, P8, W&T, K to end.
Row 5: Sl 1, P10, W&T, K to end.
Row 6: Sl 1, P12, W&T, K to end.
Row 7: Sl 1, P14, W&T, K to end.
Row 8: Sl 1, P16, W&T, K to end.
Row 9: Sl 1, P14, W&T, K to end.
Row 10: Sl 1, P12, W&T, K to end.
Row 11: Sl 1, P10, W&T, K to end.
Row 12: Sl 1, P8, W&T, K to end.
Row 13: Sl 1, P6, W&T, K to end.
Row 14: Sl 1, P4, W&T, K to end.
Row 15: Sl 1, P2, W&T, K to end.

Return held sts to needle and knit to complete the row. Continue with Ridge Pattern for another 3", ending with row 8. Remove waste yarn from cast-on edge stitch by stitch, freeing the bottom loops of your first row of knitting. Place these new stitches on a spare needle. Graft the seam together using the kitchener stitch.

Wrist Warmers

DIFFICULTY BEGINNER

YARN LANA GROSSA MEILENWEIT FANTASY (100 GRAMS)

NEEDLES US 2 (2.75 MM) *OR THE SIZE YOU NEED TO GET GAUGE*

SIZE WOMEN'S MEDIUM
MEASUREMENTS 8" HAND CIRCUMFERENCE AROUND PALM ABOVE THUMB; LENGTH: 6"

GAUGE 28 STS AND 36 ROWS = 4" IN STOCKINETTE STITCH

SHORT ROWS
Shape the thumb gusset with short rows. To prevent a hole when turning at the end of a short row, wrap a stitch as follows: with yarn to wrong side, slip next stitch to right hand needle. Bring yarn to right side and slip stitch back to left-hand needle. Turn and knit. You have wrapped the working yarn around the last unworked stitch. This is abbreviated in the instructions as W&T for wrap and turn. Because reverse stockinette is used as the right side, there is no need to pick up the wraps—they blend right in with the knitting.

You'll be surprised at how warm these little gauntlets make you feel. The sideways ridge pattern expands to fit just about any hand.

Convertible Mittens

DIFFICULTY INTERMEDIATE

YARN LANA GROSSA MEILENWEIT SCALA (100 GRAMS)

NEEDLES SET OF FOUR DOUBLE-POINTED US 2 (2.75 MM) OR THE SIZE YOU NEED TO GET GAUGE

SIZE WOMEN'S MEDIUM (MEN'S MEDIUM)
MEASUREMENTS 8" (9") HAND CIRCUMFERENCE AROUND PALM ABOVE THUMB

GAUGE 32 STS AND 44 ROWS = 4" IN STOCKINETTE STITCH

No more fumbling for your keys on a cold morning. Flip the tops back when you need your fingertips free, then pull them up for extra warmth.

Cuff
Loosely CO 64 (72) sts. Divide stitches on three needles and join into a circle, being careful not to twist your stitches. Work in K2 P2 ribbing until piece measures 3" from beginning. Change to st st and K 1 round.

Lower Palm
Set up round: K32 (36), pm, m1, pm, K32 (36).

Increase round: K to marker, sl marker, m1, K to marker, m1, sl marker, K to end of round.

Continue in st st, working increase round every 3rd round 10 times—21 (25) sts between markers, 85 (97) sts total.

Next round: K to marker, remove marker, place gusset sts on waste yarn for holding, remove marker, CO 1 st to bridge the gap, K to end of round—65 (73) sts.

For Left Hand: K34 (38), P30 (34), K1.
For Right Hand: K1, P30 (34), K34 (38).

Work even until palm measures 3¾" (4¼") above ribbing.

Little Finger
K8 (9), place next 50 (56) sts on waste yarn, CO 1 (3) st to bridge the gap, K to end of round—16 (20) sts. Arrange sts evenly on 3 needles and work 4 rounds in K2 P2 ribbing. BO loosely in ribbing.

Upper Palm

Place held sts on needles and join yarn at base of little finger. Pick up 2 sts along CO edge at base of little finger—52 (58) sts. Work in st st for 4 rounds.

Ring Finger

K9 (10), place next 34 (38) sts on waste yarn, CO 2 (4) sts to bridge the gap, K9 (10)—20 (24) sts. Arrange sts evenly on 3 needles and work 4 rounds in K2 P2 ribbing. BO loosely in ribbing.

Middle Finger

Place held sts on needles and join yarn at base of ring finger. K8 (9), place next 18 (20) sts on waste yarn, CO 2 (3) sts to bridge the gap, K8 (9), pick up 2 (3) sts along CO edge at base of ring finger—20 (24) sts. Arrange sts evenly on 3 needles and work 4 rounds in K2 P2 ribbing. BO loosely in ribbing.

Index Finger

Place remaining sts on needles. Join yarn and pick up 2 (4) sts along CO edge at base of middle finger—20 (24) sts. Arrange sts evenly on 3 needles and work 4 rounds in K2 P2 ribbing. BO loosely in ribbing.

Thumb

Place held gusset sts on needles. Join yarn and pick up 1 st at palm—22 (26) sts. Arrange sts evenly on 3 needles and work until thumb measures 1¾" (2¼").

Next round: K2tog 11 (13) times.
Next round: K2tog 4 (5) times, K3tog.

Cut yarn and draw through remaining 5 (6) sts. Pull tight and fasten off.

Mitten Top

CO 34 (38) sts. Pick up 30 (34) sts in purl bumps across back of hand—64 (72) sts. Join into a circle. Work in K2 P2 ribbing for 1". Change to st st and work for 1½" (2") more.

Shape Top

Set-up round: * K16 (18), pm, repeat from * 3 times more.

Decrease round: * K to 2 sts before marker, K2tog, repeat from * 3 times more.

Continue in st st, working decrease round every other round 8 times, then every round until 4 sts remain. Work 4-stitch knitted cord for 1½". Break yarn, fold cord in half and sew down for button loop. Sew button to cuff in position to correspond with loop when mitten top is folded back. Weave in ends and block to finished measurements.

TIP
*Leave a generous tail
when joining yarn at
the beginning of each
finger. When you
weave in these tails,
use them to close up
any little gaps that
develop at the base of
the fingers.*

Girly Fun

Girly Fun

Girly Fun

Girly Fun

Girly Fun

Girly Fun

Girly Fun

Camisole

This little camisole is extra feminine with its ruffled edges and buttons in back.

DIFFICULTY INTERMEDIATE

YARN LANA GROSSA MEILENWEIT MULTIRINGLE (200 (200, 300) GRAMS)

NEEDLES 29" CIRCULAR US 2 (2.75 MM) AND US 3 (3.25 MM) *OR THE SIZE YOU NEED TO GET GAUGE*; SET OF TWO US 3 (3.25 MM) DOUBLE-POINTED NEEDLES.

NOTIONS FIVE ½" BUTTONS

MEASUREMENTS
CHEST: 36" (38", 40")
LENGTH: 18" (18", 18")

GAUGE 28 STS AND 36 ROWS = 4" IN STOCKINETTE STITCH

Seed Stitch
Row 1: * K1, P1, repeat from * to end of row.
Row 2: Knit the purl sts and purl the knit sts as they face you.

Body
With smaller needle, CO 69 sts. Work in Seed Stitch for 10 rows. Change to larger needle and work in st st until piece measures 10" (11", 12") from beginning.

Shape Left Armhole
Continuing in st st, inc 1 st at beg of every RS row 10 times—79 sts. At beg of next RS row, CO 22 sts—101 sts.

Front
Row 1 (RS): K.
Row 2 (WS): P to last 4 sts, slip 4 as if to purl with yarn in front.

Repeat these two rows until piece measures 24" (25", 26") from beginning, ending with Row 2.

Shape Right Armhole
BO 22 sts at beg of next row. Continue in st st, dec 1 st at beg of every RS row 10 times—69 sts. Continue without shaping until piece measures 35" (37", 39") from beginning. Change to smaller needle and work in Seed Stitch for 4 rows.

Buttonhole row: K1, P1 * yo, P2tog, (K1, P1) 7 times, repeat from * to last 3 sts, end with yo, P2tog, K1.

Work in Seed Stitch for another 5 rows. BO.

Bottom Border
Using smaller needle, pick up and knit 220 (232, 244) sts along lower edge.

Row 1 and all WS rows: (P1, K1) twice, P to last 4 sts, (P1, K1) twice.

Row 2 (RS): (K1, P1) twice, * yo, K4, repeat from * to last 4 sts, (K1, P1) twice.

Row 4: (K1, P1) twice, * yo, K5, repeat from * to last 4 sts, (K1, P1) twice.

Row 6: (K1, P1) twice, * yo, K6, repeat from * to last 4 sts, (K1, P1) twice.

Row 8: (K1, P1) twice, * yo, K7, repeat from * to last 4 sts, (K1, P1) twice.

Row 10: (K1, P1) twice, * yo, K8, repeat from * to last 4 sts, (K1, P1) twice.

Row 12: (K1, P1) twice, * yo, K9, repeat from * to last 4 sts, (K1, P1) twice—544 (574, 604) sts.

Row 13: (P1, K1) twice, P to last 4 sts, (P1, K1) twice.

Row 14: K1, P1, repeat to end.

Row 15: P1, K1, repeat to end.

BO.

Top Ruffle

Using smaller needle, CO 72 sts. Work rows 1-15 as for bottom border. (You should have 174 sts at the end of row 12.) Sew ruffle to top edge of camisole just below knitted cord edge.

Left Side Border and Strap

Using larger needle, CO 4 sts. With RS facing, pick up and knit 82 (86, 90) sts along upper edge of left back and armhole—86 (90, 94) sts. At top edge of armhole, pick up sts through both layers—the ruffle and the body of the camisole. Break yarn and reattach to center back. Work knitted cord edging as follows: * K3, K2tog (last CO st together with 1st picked up st). Slip 4 sts back to left-hand needle and repeat from * until all picked up sts have been worked into cord. Continue with cord as follows: *K4, slip these sts back to left hand needle and repeat from * until cord

extends 12" beyond top front edge. BO. Sew end of cord to upper back 4" from buttonband.

Right Side Border and Strap

Using larger needle, with RS facing, pick up and knit 82 (86, 90) sts along right armhole and upper back edge. At top edge of armhole, pick up sts through both layers—the ruffle and the body of the camisole. Break yarn. Using double-pointed needles, CO 4 sts. Work knitted cord as follows: *K4, slip these sts back to left-hand needle and repeat from * until cord measures 12". Join cord to upper edge of right front and work knitted cord edging as follows: * K3, K2tog (last st together with 1st picked up st). Slip 4 sts back to left-hand needle and repeat from * until all picked up sts are worked into cord. BO. Sew end of cord to upper back 4" from buttonhole band.

Finishing

Attach buttons opposite buttonholes. Weave in ends and block to finished measurements.

> **TIP**
> *Try working your knitted cord edging with a double-pointed needle in your right hand and your picked up sts on the circular needle in your left hand.*

Socks

Socks

Socks

Socks

Socks

Socks

Socks

Ripple Socks

TIP
Even if you usually work your socks with a set of four needles, use five for this pattern. Having four needles to hold your stitches gives you two complete pattern repeats on each needle.

Ripple Pattern
Round 1: K.
Round 2: * yo, K2, dbl dec, K2, yo, K1, repeat from * to end of round.

Rep these 2 rounds.

Cuff
Loosely CO 64 sts. Arrange sts evenly on four needles and join into a circle, being careful not to twist your sts. Work 5 rows in garter st.

Leg
Change to Ripple Pattern and work until piece measures 7", ending with round 2.

Divide for Heel
K 15 sts. Slip the remaining st on needle 1 to needle 2. Turn work. Sl 1, P14, m1, P16 from needle 4. You now have 17 sts on needle 3 and 16 sts on needle 4 for your instep, and 32 sts to work for your heel flap.

Heel Flap (worked back and forth in rows)
Row 1 (RS): * Sl 1, K1, repeat from * to end of row.
Row 2: Sl 1, P to end of row.

Repeat these two rows 14 times more, then work row 1 again—31 rows.

Turn Heel
Row 1: Sl 1, P16, P2tog, P1, turn.
Row 2: Sl 1, K3, K2tog, K1, turn.
Row 3: Sl 1, P4, P2tog, P1, turn.
Row 4: Sl 1, K5, K2tog, K1, turn.
Row 5: Sl 1, P6, P2tog, P1, turn.
Row 6: Sl 1, K7, K2tog, K1, turn.
Row 7: Sl 1, P8, P2tog, P1, turn.
Row 8: Sl 1, K9, K2tog, K1, turn.
Row 9: Sl 1, P10, P2tog, P1, turn.
Row 10: Sl 1, K11, K2tog, K1, turn.
Row 11: Sl 1, P12, P2tog, P1, turn.
Row 12: Sl 1, K13, K2tog, K1, turn.
Row 13: Sl 1, P14, P2tog, P1, turn.
Row 14: Sl 1, K15, K2tog, K1 (18 sts remain).

Pick up Sts for Gussets

Continuing with the needle holding your heel sts, pick up and knit 16 sts down the left side of heel flap; using a second needle, K 33 sts at instep; using a third needle, pick up and knit 16 stitches up the right side of heel flap; K 9 sts to center of heel—83 sts. Beg of round is at center of heel.

Decrease Gussets

Round 1:
Needle 1—K to last 3 sts, K2tog, K1.
Needle 2—K1, * yo, K2, dbl dec, K2, yo, K1, repeat from * once more.
Needle 3— * yo, K2, dbl dec, K2, yo, K1, repeat from * once more.
Needle 4—K1, SSK, K to end of round.
Round 2: K.

Alternate these two rounds 8 times more—65 sts.

Foot

Maintaining Ripple Pattern on needles two and three, and working in st st on needles 1 and 4, continue without shaping until foot is 2" less then desired foot length measured from back of heel (about 8" for a women's shoe size 8). On final row, K2tog at beg of needle two—64 sts.

Shape Toe

Round 1:
Needle 1—K to last 3 sts, K2tog, K1.
Needle 2—K1, SSK, K to end.
Needle 3—K to last 3 sts, K2tog, K1.
Needle 4—K1, SSK, K to end of round.
Round 2: K.

Repeat these 2 rounds 7 times more—32 sts.

K sts on needle 1 so that yarn is coming out the side of the toe. Graft toe closed with kitchener stitch.

Most fancy stitch patterns are lost in self-striping yarn. This one works well with the stripe, particularly if your yarn style has more solid-colored stripes and few speckled areas.

Tabi Socks

Cuff

Loosely CO 64 sts. Divide sts evenly on three needles and join into a circle, being careful not to twist your sts. Work in K2 P2 ribbing for 2".

Leg

Change to st st and work until piece measures 8" from cast-on edge.

Divide for Heel

K 16 sts. Sl remaining sts on this needle to needle 2 for holding. Turn work. Sl 1, P31. Move remaining sts on this needle to needle 2 for holding. You now have 32 sts held on needle 2 for your instep, and 32 sts to work for your heel flap.

Heel Flap (worked back and forth in rows)

Row 1 (RS): * Sl 1, K1, repeat from * to end of row.
Row 2: Sl 1, P to end of row.

Repeat these two rows 14 times more, them work row 1 again—31 rows.

Turn Heel

Row 1: Sl 1, P16 (18), P2tog, P1, turn.
Row 2: Sl 1, K3, K2tog, K1, turn.
Row 3: Sl 1, P4, P2tog, P1, turn.
Row 4: Sl 1, K5, K2tog, K1, turn.
Row 5: Sl 1, P6, P2tog, P1, turn.
Row 6: Sl 1, K7, K2tog, K1, turn.
Row 7: Sl 1, P8, P2tog, P1, turn.
Row 8: Sl 1, K9, K2tog, K1, turn.
Row 9: Sl 1, P10, P2tog, P1, turn.
Row 10: Sl 1, K11, K2tog, K1, turn.
Row 11: Sl 1, P12, P2tog, P1, turn.
Row 12: Sl 1, K13, K2tog, K1, turn.
Row 13: Sl 1, P14, P2tog, P1, turn.
Row 14: Sl 1, K15, K2tog, K1 (18 sts remain).

DIFFICULTY INTERMEDIATE

YARN LANA GROSSA MEILENWEIT INCA (100 GRAMS)

NEEDLES SET OF FOUR DOUBLE-POINTED US 2 (2.75 MM) *OR THE SIZE YOU NEED TO GET GAUGE*

SIZE WOMEN'S MEDIUM
MEASUREMENTS 8" FOOT CIRCUMFERENCE

GAUGE 32 STS AND 40 ROWS = 4" IN STOCKINETTE STITCH

Add warmth to your favorite flip-flops with these fun socks. Tabi is the name of the traditional Japanese split sock.

Pick up Sts for Gussets

Continuing with the needle holding your heel sts, pick up and knit 16 sts down the left side of heel flap. Using a second needle, K 32 sts at instep. Using a third needle, pick up and knit 16 stitches up the right side of heel flap. K 9 sts to center of heel—82 sts. Beg of round is at center of heel. K one round.

Decrease Gussets

Round 1:
Needle 1—K to last 3 sts, K2tog, K1.
Needle 2—K.
Needle 3—K1, SSK, K to end of round.
Round 2: K.

Alternate these two rounds 8 times more—64 sts.

Foot

Continue without shaping until foot is 2" less then desired foot length measured from back of heel (about 8" for a women's shoe size 8).

***Right Foot

K38, place next 20 sts on waste yarn for holding, CO 4 sts to bridge the gap, K to end of round. Arrange so that there are 16 sts on each needle, with beginning of needle 1 at center of bottom of foot.

Shape Toe

Round 1:
Needle 1—K to last 3 sts, K2tog, K1.
Needle 2—K1, SSK, K to end.
Needle 3—K.
Round 2: K.

Repeat these 2 rounds until 28 sts remain.

K sts on needle 1 so that yarn is coming out the side of the toe.

Graft toe closed with kitchener stitch.

Big Toe

Return held sts to needles. Pick up 4 sts along CO edge at side of toe—24 sts. Divide sts evenly on 3 needles and work in st st for 2".

Next round: K2tog 12 times.
Next round: K2tog 6 times.

Break yarn and draw through remaining 6 sts. Pull tight and fasten off.

Left Foot

Work same as for right foot until ***. K6, place next 20 sts on waste yarn for holding, CO 4 sts to bridge the gap, K to end of round. Arrange so that there are 16 sts on each needle, with beginning of needle 1 at center of bottom of foot.

Shape Toe

Round 1:
Needle 1—K.
Needle 2—K to last 3 sts, K2tog, K1.
Needle 3—K1, SSK, K to end.
Round 2: K

Repeat these 2 rounds until 28 sts remain. On final round, K needles 1 and 2 only, so that yarn is coming out the side of the toe. Graft toe closed with kitchener stitch. Work big toe as for right foot.

> ### TIP
> *Toe lengths can vary quite a bit from person to person. If the intended foot is handy, try the sock on before you finish the toes. You can carefully slip the sock onto the wearer's foot while the stitches are still on the needles.*

Slouch Socks

DIFFICULTY INTERMEDIATE

YARN LANA GROSSA MEILENWEIT 6 MULTIEFFEKT (100 GRAMS)

NEEDLES SET OF FOUR DOUBLE-POINTED US 2 (2.75 MM) *OR THE SIZE YOU NEED TO GET GAUGE*

SIZE WOMEN'S MEDIUM (MEN'S MEDIUM)
MEASUREMENTS 8" (9") CIRCUMFERENCE

GAUGE 32 STS AND 40 ROWS = 4" IN STOCKINETTE STITCH

Cuff

Loosely CO 80 (90) sts. Arrange evenly on three needles and join into a circle, being careful not to twist your sts. Work in Spiral Rib pattern as follows:

Rounds 1-4: * K3, P2, repeat from * to end of round.
Rounds 5-8: * K2, P2, K1, repeat from * to end of round.
Rounds 9-12: *K1, P2, K2, repeat from * to end of round.
Rounds 12-16: * P2, K3, repeat from * to end of round.

The soft waves of the spiral ribbing give this sock a casual feeling.

This design is a great choice if you like a more relaxed fit through the ankle and leg.

Rounds 17-20: * P1, K3, P1, repeat from * to end of round.

Repeat these 20 rounds twice more, for a total of 60 rounds.

Decrease round: K2, * SSK, K3, repeat from * to last stitch, end with K1—64 (72) sts.

Knit 4 rounds.

Divide for Heel
K 16 (18) sts. Sl remaining sts on this needle to needle 2 for holding. Turn work. Sl 1, P31 (35). Move remaining sts on this needle to needle 2 for holding. You now have 32 (36) sts held on needle 2 for your instep, and 32 (36) sts to work for your heel flap.

Heel Flap (worked back and forth in rows)
Row 1 (RS): * Sl 1, K1, repeat from * to end of row.
Row 2: Sl 1, P to end of row.

Repeat these two rows 14 (16) times more, then work row 1 again—31 (35) rows.

Turn Heel
Row 1: Sl 1, P16 (18), P2tog, P1, turn.
Row 2: Sl 1, K3, K2tog, K1, turn.
Row 3: Sl 1, P4, P2tog, P1, turn.
Row 4: Sl 1, K5, K2tog, K1, turn.
Row 5: Sl 1, P6, P2tog, P1, turn.
Row 6: Sl 1, K7, K2tog, K1, turn.
Row 7: Sl 1, P8, P2tog, P1, turn.
Row 8: Sl 1, K9, K2tog, K1, turn.
Row 9: Sl 1, P10, P2tog, P1, turn.
Row 10: Sl 1, K11, K2tog, K1, turn.
Row 11: Sl 1, P12, P2tog, P1, turn.
Row 12: Sl 1, K13, K2tog, K1, turn.
Row 13: Sl 1, P14, P2tog, P1, turn.
Row 14: Sl 1, K15, K2tog, K1. For first size, 18 sts remain. Go to *Pick up Sts for Gussets*. For second size, continue with rows 15 and 16.

Row 15: Sl 1, P16, P2tog, P1, turn.
Row 16: Sl 1, K17, K2tog, K1—20 sts remain.

Pick up Sts for Gussets
Continuing with the needle holding your heel sts, pick up and knit 16 (18) sts down the left side of heel flap. Using a second needle, K 32 (36) sts at instep. Using a third needle, pick up and knit 16 (18) stitches up the right side of heel flap. K 9 sts to center of heel—82 (92) sts. Beg of round is at center of heel. K one round.

Decrease Gussets
Round 1:
Needle 1—K to last 3 sts, K2tog, K1.
Needle 2—K.
Needle 3—K1, SSK, K to end of round.
Round 2: K.

Alternate these two rounds 8 (9) times more—64 (72) sts.

Foot
Continue without shaping until foot is 2" less then desired foot length measured from back of heel (about 8" for a women's shoe size 8, 9" for a men's size 10).

Shape Toe
Round 1:
Needle 1—K to last 3 sts, K2tog, K1.
Needle 2—K1, SSK, K to last 3 sts, K2tog, K1.
Needle 3—K1, SSK, K to end of round.
Round 2: K.

Repeat these 2 rounds 7 (8) times more—32 (36) sts. K sts on needle 1 so that yarn is coming out the side of the toe. Graft toe closed with kitchener stitch.

Scarves

Scarves

Scarves

Scarves

Scarves

Chevron Stripe Scarf

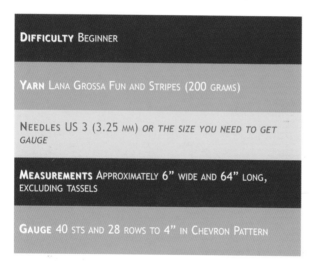

DIFFICULTY BEGINNER

YARN LANA GROSSA FUN AND STRIPES (200 GRAMS)

NEEDLES US 3 (3.25 MM) *OR THE SIZE YOU NEED TO GET GAUGE*

MEASUREMENTS APPROXIMATELY 6" WIDE AND 64" LONG, EXCLUDING TASSELS

GAUGE 40 STS AND 28 ROWS TO 4" IN CHEVRON PATTERN

Let the stripes zig zag across your scarf. This pattern forms points at both ends, marking the perfect spots for tassels.

Chevron Pattern (Multiple of 15 sts)
Row 1 (WS): K.
Row 2 (RS): * K2tog, K5, m1, K1, m1, K5, SSK, repeat from * to end of row.

Repeat Rows 1 and 2.

Scarf
Loosely CO 60 sts. Work in Chevron Pattern until piece measures approximately 64". BO loosely.

Finishing
Weave in ends and block to finished measurements. Make 9 tassels and attach one to each point on ends of scarf.

Serpentine Scarf

DIFFICULTY BEGINNER

YARN LANA GROSSA MEILENWEIT MAGICO (200 GRAMS)

NEEDLES US 3 (3.25 MM) *OR SIZE YOU NEED TO GET GAUGE*

MEASUREMENTS APPROX 7" WIDE AND 65" LONG, EXCLUDING FRINGE.

GAUGE 28 STS AND 50 ROWS = 4" IN GARTER STITCH

Scarf
Loosely CO 42 sts.

Rows 1-4: Sl 1, K to end of row.
Row 5: Sl 1, K36, W&T, K to end of row.
Row 6: Sl 1, K31, W&T, K to end of row.
Row 7: Sl 1, K26, W&T, K to end of row.
Row 8: Sl 1, K21, W&T, K to end of row.
Row 9: Sl 1, K16, W&T, K to end of row.
Row 10: Sl 1, K11, W&T, K to end of row.
Row 11: Sl 1, K6, W&T, K to end of row.

Rows 12-15: Sl 1, K to end of row.

Row 16: Sl 1, K6, W&T, K to end of row.
Row 17: Sl 1, K11, W&T, K to end of row.
Row 18: Sl 1, K16, W&T, K to end of row.
Row 19: Sl 1, K21, W&T, K to end of row.
Row 20: Sl 1, K26, W&T, K to end of row.
Row 21: Sl 1, K31, W&T, K to end of row.
Row 22: Sl 1, K36, W&T, K to end of row.
Row 23: Sl 1, K to end of row.

Rows 24-45: Repeat rows 1-22.

Rows 46-67: Repeat rows 1-22 again.

Row 68: Sl 1, K to end of row.

Rows 69-90: Repeat rows 1-22.

Repeat these 90 rows 6 times more. BO loosely.

Finishing
For fringe, cut 84 strands each 10" long. Tie groups of two strands to every other stitch along both ends of scarf.

TIP
To highlight the wedge shapes in this scarf, you may want to wind off some yarn so an eye-catching color falls on rows 1-4 and 12-15. In the sample shown, speckled sections were used for these rows, outlining the solid-colored wedges.

Short rows form wedges that bend this scarf into playful curves

For the Home

For the Home

For the Home

For the Home

For the Home

Four Pillows

DIFFICULTY BEGINNER

YARN LANA GROSSA MEILENWEIT FANTASY (100 GRAMS FOR EACH PILLOW)

NEEDLES TWO 29" CIRCULAR US 3 (3.25 MM) FOR SQUARE PILLOWS; ONE 16" CIRCULAR US 3 (3.25 MM) FOR BOLSTER PILLOW *OR THE SIZE YOU NEED TO GET GAUGE*

NOTIONS AND OTHER MATERIALS SPLIT RING MARKER. 14" SQUARE PILLOW FORM FOR SQUARE PILLOWS. 6" x 14" NECK ROLL PILLOW FORM FOR BOLSTER PILLOW.

MEASUREMENTS SQUARE PILLOWS = 14" x 14". BOLSTER PILLOW = 6" x 14"

GAUGE 28 STS AND 36 ROWS = 4" IN STOCKINETTE STITCH

This lively collection of pillows will add a spark to your sofa or window seat.

Seed Stitch
Row 1: * K1, P1, repeat from * to end of row.
Row 2: Knit the purl sts and purl the knit sts as they face you.

Bolster Pillow
Using 16" circular needle, loosely cast on 120 sts. Work in Seed Stitch for 2". Knit 1 round.

Eyelet round: * K4, K2tog, yo, repeat from * to end of round.

Change to st st and work until piece measures 21" from beginning. Repeat eyelet round. Knit 1 round. Change to Seed Stitch and work for 2" more. BO loosely. Make 2 knitted cords 10" long. Insert pillow form. Thread a knitted cord through each set of eyelets, pull tight and tie in a small bow.

Pinwheel Pillow
Using 29" circular needle, CO 40 sts. Work in garter stitch for 79 rows—40 ridges. * BO until 1 st remains. With RS facing, pick up and knit 39 sts along left side of square—40 sts. Work in garter stitch for 79 rows—40 ridges. Repeat from * twice more. BO all sts. Sew side of final square to CO edge of first square.

Cross Pillow
Using 29" circular needle, CO 79 sts. Mark center st with split ring marker or safety pin.

Row 1 (WS): Sl 1, K to end of row.
Row 2 (RS): Sl 1, K to 1 st before marked st, dbl dec, K to end of row.

Repeat these two rows until 3 sts remain. K3 together and fasten off. Make 3 more squares. Sew cast on edges together as shown in diagram.

Diamond Pillow
Using 29" circular needle, CO 3 sts.

Next row: Sl 1, m1, K to end of row.

Repeat this row until there are 58 sts on your needle.

Next row: Sl 1, K2tog, K to end of row.

Repeat this row until 3 sts remain. BO. Make 3 more squares. Sew squares together as shown in diagram.

Pillow Backs and Finishing for all Square Pillows
Pillow Back: Using 29" circular needle, CO 80 sts. Work in st st for 14". BO.

Finishing: Using 29" circular needle, pick up 80 sts along each side of pillow front—320 sts. Using another 29" circular needle, pick up 80 sts along each side of pillow back. With WS's together, join front to back with 3-needle bind off. When 3 sides are bound off, insert pillow form. Continue with 3-needle bind off on 4th side, encasing form in pillow cover.

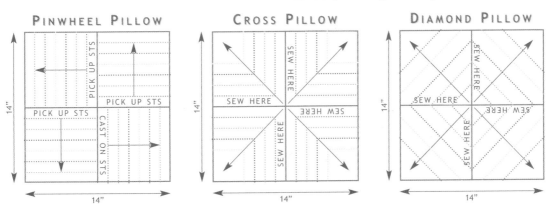

ARROWS INSIDE BLOCKS INDICATE DIRECTION TO KNIT

Choose colors to coordinate with your decor, or add a bright and playful accent.

Hot Water Bottle Cover

DIFFICULTY BEGINNER

YARN LANA GROSSA MEILENWEIT MULTIEFFEKT (100 GRAMS)

NEEDLES 16" CIRCULAR AND SET OF 4 DOUBLE-POINTED US 3 (3.25 MM) *OR THE SIZE YOU NEED TO GET GAUGE*; 16" CIRCULAR AND SET OF 4 DOUBLE-POINTED US 2 (2.75 MM)

NOTIONS STITCH MARKERS

MEASUREMENTS 7½" WIDE X 10½" HIGH, EXCLUDING NECK

GAUGE 28 STS AND 36 ROWS = 4" IN STOCKINETTE STITCH

Hot Water Bottle Cover

Using smaller circular needle, CO 54 sts. Working back and forth in rows, work K2 P2 ribbing for 2". Place a marker on the needle. Use cable cast-on method to CO 54 more sts. Join into the round, being careful not to twist sts. Place marker of a different color to mark beginning of round. Work K2 P2 ribbing for 1" more. Change to larger needle and work in st st until piece measures 8" above ribbing.

Shape "Shoulders"

Next round: * K2, SSK, K to 4 sts before marker, K2tog, K2, slip marker, repeat from * once more.

Repeat this row until 56 sts remain, changing to double-pointed needles when necessary.

"Neck"

Change to smaller double-pointed needles and work K2 P2 ribbing for 1".

Next round: * K1, m1, K1, P2, repeat from * to end of round.

Work 4 rounds in K3 P2 ribbing.

Next round: * K3, P1, m1, P1, repeat from * to end of round.

Work 4 rounds in K3 P3 ribbing. BO.

Finishing

Fold ribbed flap up to inside of cover. Sew sides of flap to inside of cover to make pocket.

Make your hot water bottle extra cozy with this fitted cover. If you use a cheery colorway, your bottle won't get lost in the bed covers!

Small Pet Bed

DIFFICULTY INTERMEDIATE

YARN LANA GROSSA MEILENWEIT SCALA (200 GRAMS)

NEEDLES 16" AND 24" CIRCULAR AND SET OF FOUR DOUBLE-POINTED US 3 (3.25 MM) *OR THE SIZE YOU NEED TO GET GAUGE*

ACCESSORIES STITCH MARKER
2" THICK HIGH-DENSITY FOAM, 14" DIAMETER
1" THICK HIGH-DENSITY FOAM, 4" x 32"

MEASUREMENTS APPROX. 15" DIAMETER AND 4" HIGH

GAUGE 28 STS AND 36 ROWS = 4" IN STOCKINETTE STITCH

Bed Cushion

Using longer circular needle, CO 42 sts.

Row 1 and all WS rows: Sl 1, K to end.
Row 2: Sl 1, K to last 3 sts, K2tog, K1.

Repeat these two rows until 3 sts remain.

Next row (WS): Sl 1, K2.
Next row: Sl 1, K2tog.
Next row: Sl 1, P1.
Next row: K2tog—1 st remains.

With RS facing, pick up and knit 41 sts along diagonal edge—42 sts.

Repeat from row 1 until 6 wedges are complete. Fasten off last stitch. Sew cast-on edge to final diagonal edge.

Using longer circular needle, pick up and knit 1 st in every ridge around edge of piece—252 sts. Place marker to indicate beginning of round. Work in st st for 4 rounds.

Next round: BO 84 sts, K to end of round.
Next round: CO 84 sts (use cable cast-on method), K to end of round.

Work in st st for 4 rounds.

Shape Underside of Cushion (Shown on P. 71)
Change to smaller circular needles and then double-pointed needles when necessary.

Row 1: * K19, K2tog, repeat from * to end of round.
Rows 2 and 3: K.
Row 4: K9, * K2tog, K18, repeat from * to last 11 sts, end K2tog, K9.
Rows 5 and 6: K.
Row 7: K12, * K2tog, K17, repeat from * to last 7 sts, end K2tog, K5.
Rows 8 and 9: K.
Row 10: K5, * K2tog, K16, repeat from * to last 13 sts, end K2tog, K11.
Rows 11 and 12: K.
Row 13: * K15, K2tog, repeat from * to end of round.
Rows 14 and 15: K.
Row 16: K8, * K2tog, K14, repeat from * to last 8 sts, end K2tog, K6.
Rows 17 and 18: K.
Row 19: K4, * K2tog, K13, repeat from * to last 11 sts, end K2tog, K9.
Rows 20 and 21: K.

Give your little dog or kitty a cozy nest to curl up in. Maybe he'll leave your yarn basket alone!

Not recommended for large breeds!

Row 22: K10, * K2tog, K12, repeat from * to last 4sts, end K2tog, K2.
Rows 23 and 23: K.
Row 25: K5, * K2tog, K11, repeat from * to last 8 sts, end K2tog, K6.
Rows 26 and 27: K.
Row 28: K2, * K2tog, K10, repeat from * to last 10 sts, end K2tog, K8.
Rows 29 and 30: K.
Row 31: K8, * K2tog, K9, repeat from * to last 3 sts, end K2tog, K1.
Rows 32 and 33: K.
Row 34: K3, * K2tog, K8, repeat from * to last 7 sts, end K2tog, K5.
Rows 35 and 36: K.
Row 37: * K7, K2tog, repeat from * to end of round.
Rows 38 and 39: K.
Row 40: K3, * K2tog, K6, repeat from * to last 5 sts, end K2tog, K3.
Rows 41 and 42: K.
Row 43: * K2tog, K5, repeat from * to end of round.
Rows 44 and 45: K.
Row 46: K2, * K2tog, K4, repeat from * to last 4 sts, end K2tog, K2.
Rows 47 and 48: K.
Row 49: * K2tog, K3, repeat from * to end of round.
Rows 50 and 51: K.
Row 52: K1, * K2tog, K2, repeat from * to last 3 sts, end K2tog, K2.
Rows 53 and 54: K.
Row 55: * K1, K2tog, repeat from * to end of round.
Rows 56 and 57: K.
Row 58: K2tog 12 times—12 sts.

Break yarn, draw through remaining 12 sts, pull tight and fasten off. Insert foam circle and sew opening closed.

Bed Back

Using double pointed needles, CO 26 sts. Starting with a purl row, work in st st for 8 rows. With RS facing, pick up and knit 6 sts along side of piece, 26 sts from cast-on edge, and 6 sts from other side—64 sts. Place a marker to indicate beginning of round. Arrange sts on three needles and work in st st until the tube is 32" long.

Next round: K26, BO 38 sts.

Working back and forth in rows, continue in st st on remaining 26 sts for 8 rows. Bind off. Insert foam strip and sew end closed. Sew bed back around cushion.

TIP
To insert the foam strip into the knitted tube, turn the tube inside out, fit the strip against the end of the tube, and roll the tube up the length of the strip.

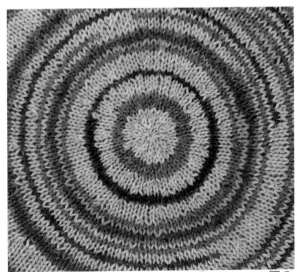

Also from Unicorn Books and Crafts

Not *just* Socks

Sandi Rosner

Now in Reprint!

UNICORN
BOOKS AND CRAFTS, INC.

Lana Grossa Meilenweit Sock Yarn
Yarn Styles and Colors Used

Project	Shown on Page	Yarn Style/Color
Beret	16	Mega Boots Stretch/703
Bias Hat	11, 12	Fantasy/4770
Button Gloves	3, 19, 24, 27	Inca/1522
Camisole	35, 36, 39	Multiringle/5110
Chevron Stripe Scarf	53, 55	Fun and Stripes/630
Convertible Mittens	30, 32, 33	Scala/6536
Four Pillows	61, 62, 64-65	Fantasy/4750
Jughead's Hat	15, 75	Scala/6534
Hot Water Bottle Cover	67	Multieffekt/3090
Ripple Socks	4, 43, 44	Magico/2521
Sawtooth Mittens	20, 22-23	Magico/2526
Serpentine Scarf	56, 58-59	Magico/2525
Slouch Socks	41, 50	Multieffekt/3080
Small Pet Bed	69, 70, 71	Scala/6535
Tabi Socks	47, 48	Inca/1527
Wrist Warmers	7, 29	Fantasy/4830

Lana Grossa Meilenweit sock yarns are available at fine knitting stores.

For a store near you, call Unicorn Books and Crafts at 1-800-289-9276.

Abbreviations

beg—beginning

BO—bind off

CO—cast on

dec—decrease

dbl dec (double decrease)—sl 2 sts together as if to knit them together, k1, pass 2 slipped sts over the knit stitch.

garter stitch—when working in rows, knit every row; when working in rounds, alternate knit and purl rounds.

inc—increase

K—knit

K2tog—knit 2 stitches together

K3tog—knit 3 stitches together

knitted cord—with 4 sts on needle, K4, *do not turn; push sts to opposite end of needle, bring yarn across back of stitches and K4; rep from * until desired length.

m1 (make 1)—use the tip of your left needle to lift up the strand running between the stitch just worked and the next stitch; knit into the back of this strand, twisting the loop to avoid making a hole.

pm—place marker

P—purl

psso—pass the slipped stitch over the st just knitted

RS—right side

sl—slip

SSK (slip, slip, knit)—slip 1 st as if to knit; slip another st as if to knit; slip both sts back to left-hand needle and knit them together through back loop.

st st (stockinette stitch)—when working in rows, knit the right side rows and purl the wrong side rows; when working in the round, knit every round.

st(s)—stitch(es)

W&T (wrap and turn)—Used to prevent holes at the turning point in short rows. With yarn in back, sl next st to right-hand needle, bring yarn to front, sl st back to left-hand needle and turn the piece, ready to work back in the other direction.

WS—wrong side

yo (inc)—yarn over needle